READING/WRITING COMPANION

Mc
Graw
Hill
Education

Cover: Nathan Love, Erwin Madrid

mheducation.com/prek-12

Send all inquiries to:
McGraw-Hill Education
Two Penn Plaza
New York, NY 10121

ISBN: 978-0-07-901794-9
MHID: 0-07-901794-0

Printed in the United States of America.

11 LMN 23

D

Welcome to Wonders!

Read exciting Literature, Science, and Social Studies texts!

★ LEARN about the world around you!

★ THINK, SPEAK, and WRITE about genres!

★ COLLABORATE in discussions and inquiry!

★ EXPRESS yourself!

my.mheducation.com
Use your student login to read texts and practice phonics, spelling, grammar, and more!

Unit 3 Changes Over Time

The Big Idea

Week 1 • What Time Is It?

Digital Tools Find this eBook and other resources at: my.mheducation.com

Week 2 • Watch It Grow!

Week 3 • Tales Over Time

Week 4 • Now and Then

(bkgd) North Wind Picture Archives; (title bkgd) DAJ/Getty Images

Week 5 • From Farm to Table

Writing and Grammar

Wrap Up the Unit

Changes Over Time

 Listen to and think about the poem "Changes, Changes."

 Talk about the girl in the picture. What can she do that she could not do when she was younger?

The Big Idea

What can happen over time?

Talk About It

Essential Question **How do we measure time?**

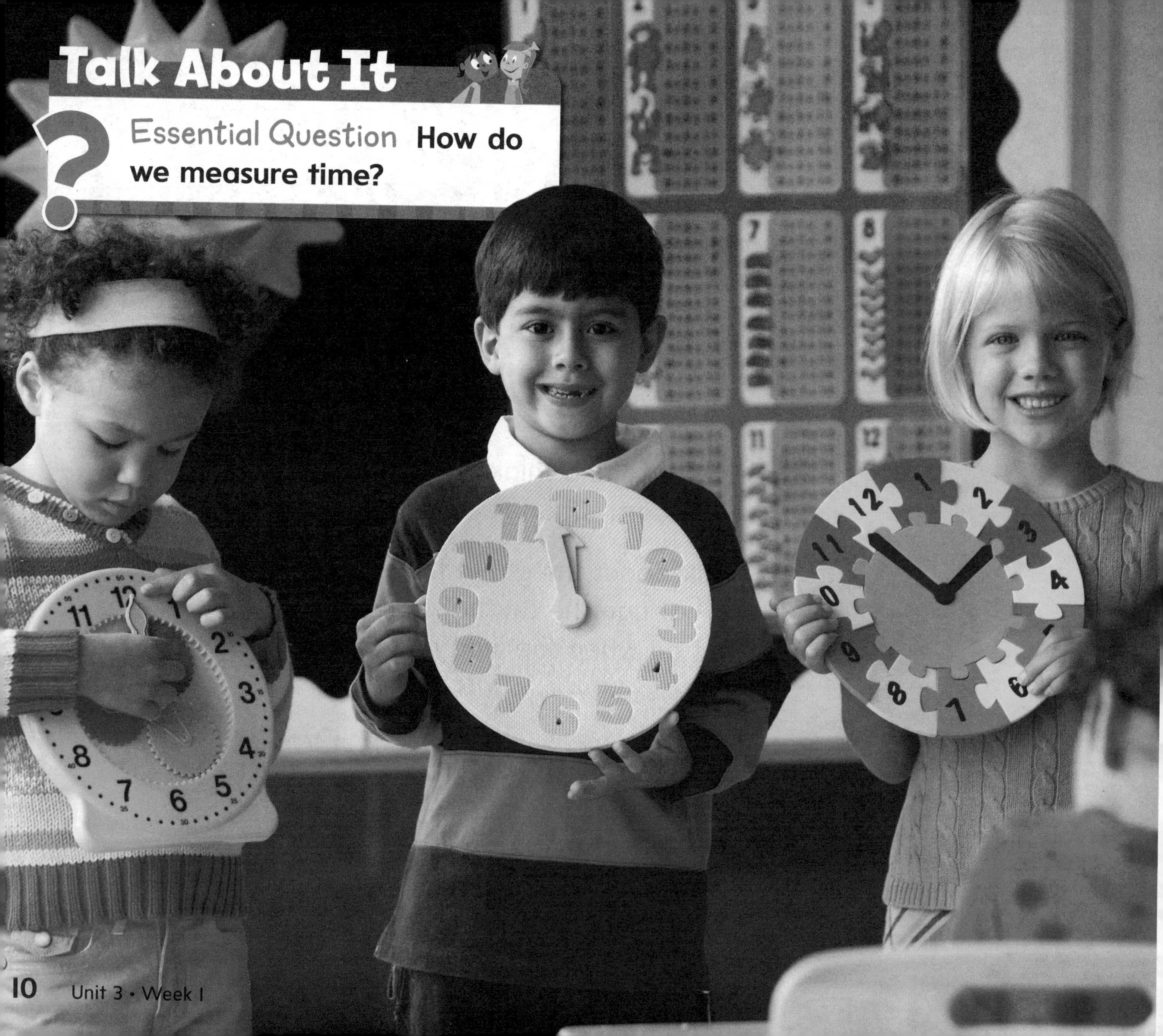

Talk about what these children are using to tell time.

Write other ways you know of to tell time.

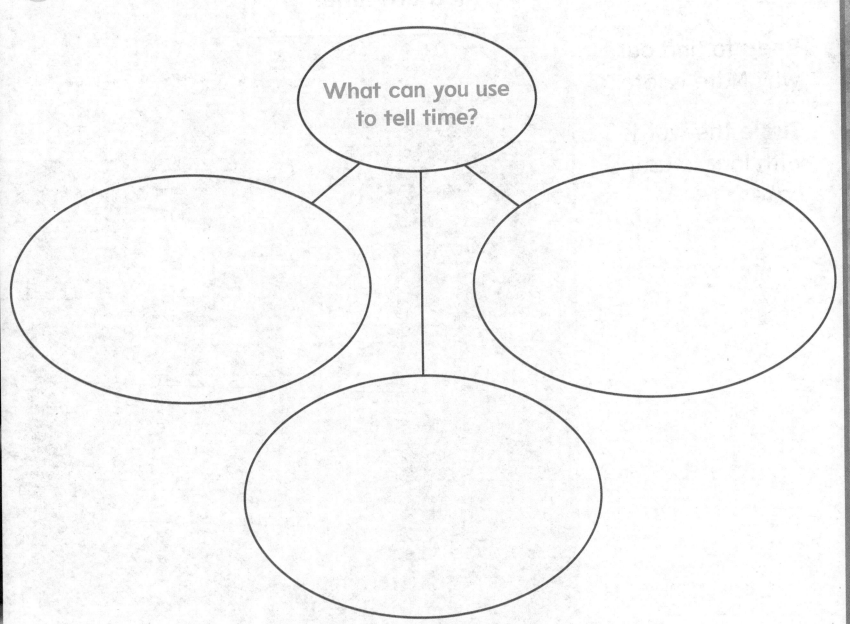

What can you use to tell time?

Shared Read

Find Text Evidence

 Read to find out why Nate is late.

 Circle the words with long *a* as in *cake*.

Essential Question

? How do we measure time?

Nate the Snake Is Late

Fantasy

Shared Read

 Talk about why Nate does not want to be late. What does this tell you about him?

 Talk about why Nate is not worried about the time on page 15.

It is 8 o'clock, and I can not be late.

I do not wish to make my pals wait.

I must be there at half past ten.

But I have lots of time until then.

Find Text Evidence

 Underline and read aloud the words *way, some,* and *away.*

 Talk about what Nate is doing. Predict what will happen because of his actions.

At last I am set and on my way there.

But I think I still have some time to spare.

I wade in this lake as frogs hop away.

I do not think they wish to play!

Shared Read

 Circle the words with long *a* as in *cake*.

 Talk about your prediction. Was it correct? Do you need to change it?

The sun is hot, and I nap on a rock.

Then I wake up and gaze at the clock.

Drats! It is 10 o'clock. Can it be?

Will my pals still be there for me?

Shared Read

 Find Text Evidence

 Underline and read aloud the words *why, now,* and *today.*

 Retell the story using the pictures and words from the story.

I dash up a lane and past the gate.

I am on my way, but am I late?

My six best pals sit with Miss Tate.

I tell them all why I am late.

They grin at me and then they say,
"Now we can hear the story today!"

A **fantasy** story has made-up characters. Fantasy stories can be told in first-person using the words *I, me, my,* and *we.*

 Reread to find out who is telling this fantasy story.

 Talk about who is telling the story and how you know.

 Write the words that tell you who is telling the story. Draw the character.

Words That Tell	Character

A **character** is the person or animal in a story. The **setting** is where and when a story takes place. The **plot** is what happens in the beginning, middle, and end of a story.

 Reread "Nate the Snake Is Late."

 Talk about what happens in the beginning of the story.

 Write about the plot of the story.

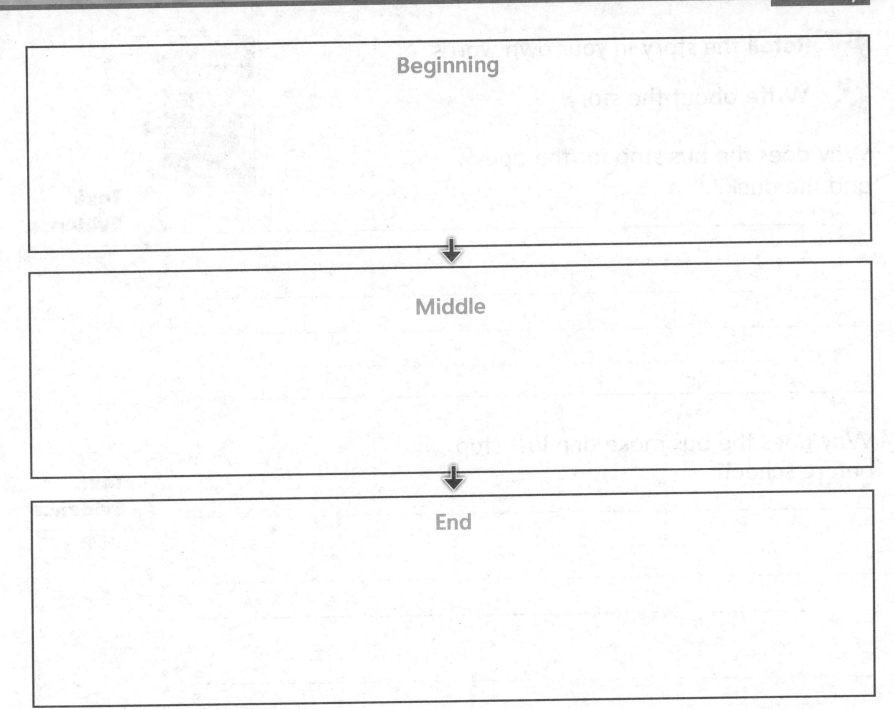

Beginning

Middle

End

Retell the story in your own words.

Write about the story.

On My Way to School
by Wong Herbert Yee

Why does the bus stop for the apes and the duck?

_____

- -

_____

- -

_____

Text Evidence

Page

Why does the bus make one last stop before school?

_____

- -

_____

- -

_____

Text Evidence

Page

Talk about how the stories are the same and different.

 Write about the stories.

How are the boy and Nate alike?

_____

_____

_____

Why might you tell the same kind of story as the boy if you were late for school?

_____

_____

_____

- -

_____

Make Inferences

Use details and what you know to figure out why the boy tells the story.

How would you feel if you were late?

Talk about what is happening on page 10.

Write two clues that help you know who tells the story.

Clue from Text	Clue from Pictures

How does the author let you know who is telling the story?

_____

- -

_____

_____

- -

_____

Talk about the sentences with rhyming words on pages 12–13.

 Write pairs of rhyming words from the story.

Page 12	Page 13

What feeling does the story have because of the rhyming words?

_____

- -

_____

- -

_____

Talk about the things that happen in the story on page 18.

 Write about two of the things that happen.

1.

2.

How do you know the boy made these things up?

_____
- -
_____
_____
- -
_____

 Write About It

Write another page for the story. Tell the excuse the boy might give his mom for getting home late.

It's About Time!

Some clocks have faces with hands. The hands point to the numbers. Some clocks have just numbers.

7:00

All clocks tell the hour and minute. There are 60 minutes in an hour. There are 60 seconds in a minute.

Read to find out about telling time.

Underline the sentence that explains how all clocks are the same.

Talk about how the clocks are different.

(t)McGraw-Hill Education; (b)Stockbyte/Getty Images

What Time Is It? **31**

Long ago, people didn't have clocks. They used the Sun to tell time instead. Tools like sundials helped them. The Sun's shadow showed the hour. But people had to guess the minutes. What time is this sundial showing?

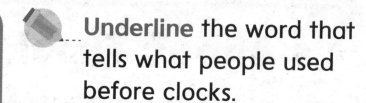

Underline the word that tells what people used before clocks.

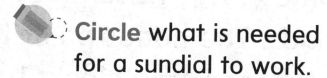

Circle what is needed for a sundial to work.

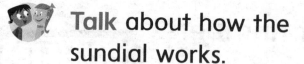

Talk about how the sundial works.

David J. Green/Alamy

Quick Tip

Look at the Sun's shadow in the photo. What will happen when the Sun moves?

Talk about the information in the text.

 Write what the facts are mostly about on pages 31 and 32.

Page 31	Page 32

Why is "It's About Time!" a good title for this text?

_____

- -

_____

- -

_____

Talk About It

What does the author want you to know after reading this text?

Tell Me About Your Day

Step 1 Pick a classmate to ask about his or her usual day.

_____

- -

_____

Step 2 Decide what you want to know about your classmate's day. Write your questions.

_____

- -

_____

_____

- -

_____

_____

- -

_____

Step 3 Ask your questions.

Step 4 Write what you learned about each part of your classmate's day.

Parts of My Classmate's Day	What Usually Happens

Step 5 Choose how to present your work.

Talk about why the bird in this poem says what he says.

Compare this poem to the beginning of *On My Way to School.*

Time to Rise

A birdie with a yellow bill
Hopped upon my window sill,
Cocked his shining eye and said:
"Ain't you 'shamed, you
sleepy-head!"

— Robert Louis Stevenson

What I Know Now

Think about the texts you heard and read this week about time. Write what you learned.

_____

- -

_____

_____

- -

_____

_____

- -

_____

 Think about what else you would like to learn about time. Talk about your ideas.

 Share one thing you learned this week about fantasy stories.

Talk About It

Essential Question How do plants change as they grow?

Talk about what you see in this photo.

Write what you know about what plants need to grow.

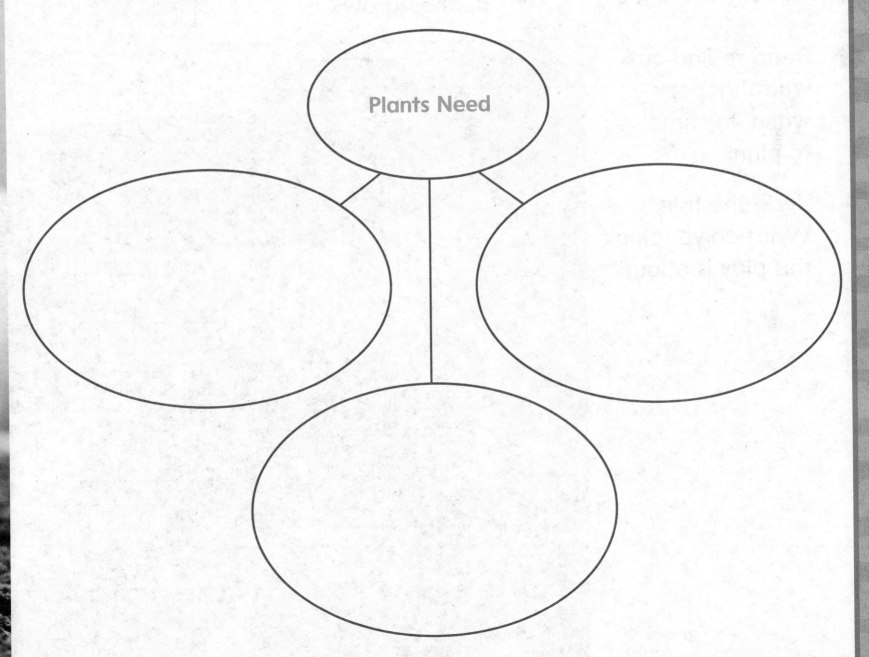

Plants Need

Masterfile

Shared Read

 Find Text Evidence

 Read to find out what happens when it is time to plant.

 Read the title. What do you think this play is about?

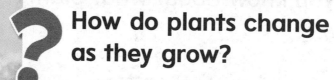

Essential Question

? How do plants change as they grow?

Time to Plant!

Shared Read

 Find Text Evidence

 Talk about what the characters say. Make a prediction about what will happen next.

 Underline and read aloud the word *together*.

Cast

Beth

Mike

Gramps

Dad

Mom

Miss White

Narrator

Beth: Dad, can we plant a garden?

Dad: Yes! That will be fine!

Gramps: We can plant vegetables.

Mike: Yum! Let's do it together.

Shared Read

 Find Text Evidence

 Underline and read aloud the words *green, water,* and *grow.*

 Think about what the characters say. Talk about your prediction. Correct it if you need to.

Mom:	Dad and I will dig.
Mike:	I will drop in five seeds.
Gramps:	I will set in green plants.
Beth:	And I will get water!

Narrator: Days pass. The Sun shines. Rain plinks and plunks.

Beth: I can spot buds on the vines!

Dad: Sun and water made them grow.

Read

Shared Read

 Find Text Evidence

 Underline and read aloud the word *should*.

 Circle the words with long *i* as in *bike*.

Narrator: Days pass. The Sun shines. Rain drips and drops.

Beth: The vegetables got big!

Dad: We should pick them.

Mom: Yes, it's time!

Play

Mike: I like to munch while I pick. I will take a bite. Yum!

Gramps: Sun and water made them ripe.

Shared Read

🔍 **Find Text Evidence**

 Talk about Beth and Mike. Did they get what they expected?

 Retell the story using the pictures and words from the story.

Narrator: They pick piles and piles.

Beth: Yikes! That's a lot!

Mike: We can't eat them all.

Gramps: I think I have a plan.

Mike: This bag is for you.

Miss White: They are such pretty vegetables! Thank you!

Beth: Sun and water made them grow.

A **play** is a genre. A play is a story that is meant to be performed. It has dialogue, or words that characters speak, and a setting.

 Reread to find out what makes this story a play.

 Talk about how you know it is a play. Then describe the setting.

 Write something you learn about Beth and Mike from the dialogue.

Character	What I Learned From the Dialogue

Events in a story or play happen in a certain order, or sequence. The main events are the plot of the story.

 Reread "Time to Plant!"

 Talk about what happens first, next, then, and last in the play.

 Write what happens in the correct sequence.

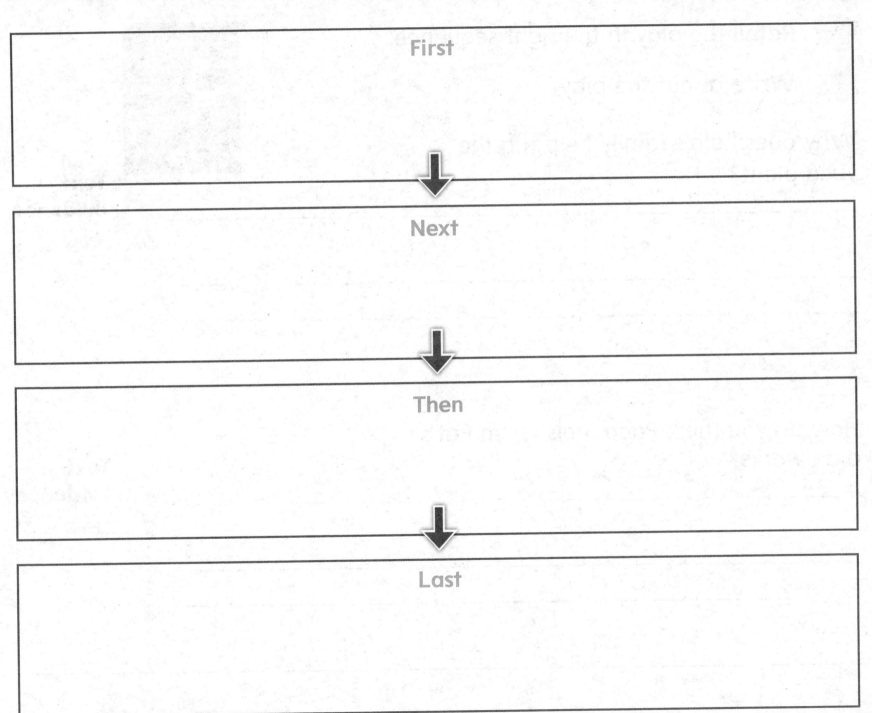

First

Next

Then

Last

Retell the play in the right sequence.

Write about the play.

Why does Lola's family help tug the yuca plant?

_____

- -

_____

- -

_____

Text Evidence

Page

How do you think Paco feels when Rat's plan works?

_____

- -

_____

- -

_____

Text Evidence

Page

Talk about how the plays are the same and different.

 Write about the plays.

How are Beth and Lola surprised in each play?

_____

- -

_____

- -

_____

Which surprise would you rather have? Why?

_____

- -

_____

- -

Make Inferences

Use clues in the dialogue to figure out what surprises Beth and Lola.

After picking vegetables, Beth says, . . .

When Lola tries to tug the yuca, she says, . . .

Talk about what Rat says on page 41.

Write what you know about Rat.

When . . .	it helps me know . . .
Rat says:	

How does the dialogue help you learn about the characters?

_____

_____

_____

_____

Write About It

What else might Rat say? In your writer's notebook, write more lines for Rat to say at the end of the play.

How Plants Grow

When a seed is planted, a root grows down in the soil. The root holds the seed in the soil. It takes in water, too.

The stem grows up from the seed. When it pops out of the soil, it is called a sprout. Green leaves grow on the stem.

 Read to find out how plants grow.

 Underline two ways that the root helps a plant.

 Talk about how the photo helps you understand the meaning of the word *sprout*.

Quick Tip

You can use the photos to help you understand the meaning of words you don't know in the text.

Nic Miller/Organics image library/Alamy

Over time, blossoms pop up on the plant. These blossoms are the plant's flowers. They can grow into a fruit such as this pumpkin. Many fruits can grow on one plant vine.

Inside the fruit are seeds. These seeds can be used to grow new plants.

blossom

fruit

msgrafixx/Shutterstock.com

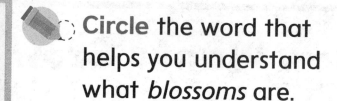 **Circle** the word that helps you understand what *blossoms* are.

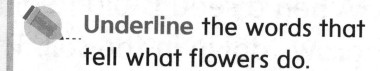 **Underline** the words that tell what flowers do.

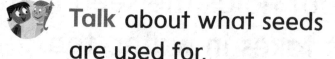 **Talk** about what seeds are used for.

Quick Tip

You can use the text and the information in the photo to understand the meaning of a word.

Talk about the sequence of the text.

 Write the sequence.

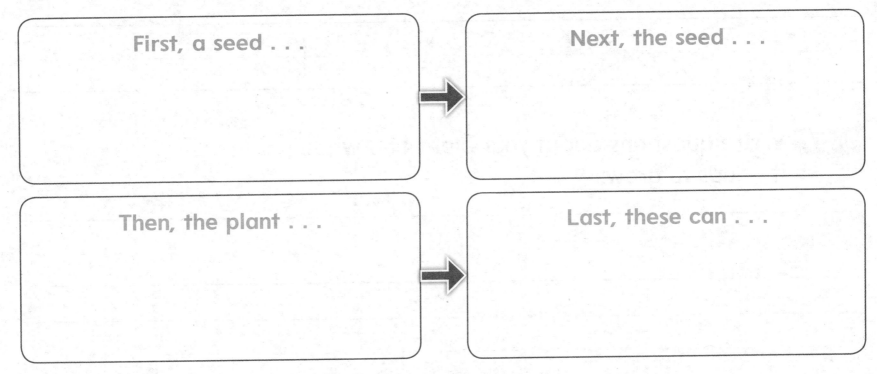

First, a seed . . .

Next, the seed . . .

Then, the plant . . .

Last, these can . . .

How is the information in this text organized?

_____

- -

_____

_____

- -

_____

Research and Inquiry

From Seed to Plant

Step 1 **Pick** a plant to research.

_____

- -

_____

Step 2 **Write** questions about your plant and what
it needs to grow.

_____

- -

_____

- -

_____

- -

_____

Step 3 **Find** books or websites with the information
you need. Read for answers to your questions.

Step 4 **List** what you learned about your plant's needs.

_____

- -

_____

- -

_____

- -

_____

- -

_____

- -

_____

- -

_____

Step 5 **Draw** your plant and label the parts.

Step 6 **Choose** how to present your work.

Talk about why *The Life of a Pomegranate* would be a good title for this painting.

 Compare a pomegranate to the other plants you read about this week.

Quick Tip

Compare using these sentence starters:

A pomegranate has . . .

Other plants also have . . .

This painting shows pomegranate seeds, tree, blossoms, and fruit.

What I Know Now

Think about the texts you heard and read this week about plants. Write what you learned.

_____

- -

_____

_____

- -

_____

_____

- -

_____

 Think about what else you would like to learn about plants. Talk about your ideas.

 Share one thing you learned this week about plays.

Talk About It

Essential Question What is a folktale?

Talk about story characters these children might be pretending to be.

 Write the names of some characters in folktales you know.

Folktale	Characters

Shared Read

 Read to find out what makes the mitten nice.

 Point to and read aloud each word in the title.

Essential Question

? **What is a folktale?**

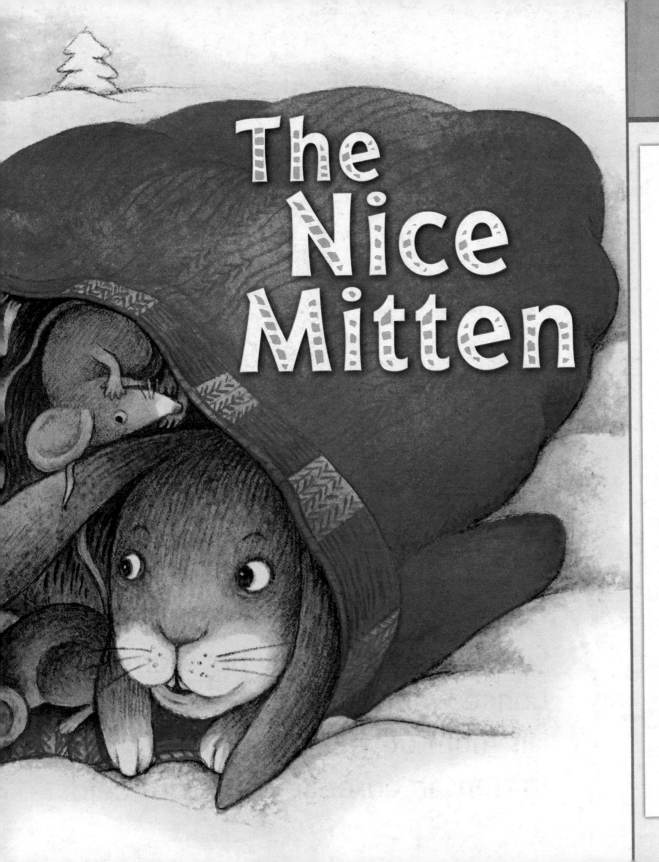

The Nice Mitten

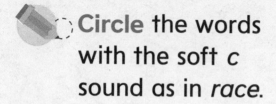 **Find Text Evidence**

Circle the words with the soft *c* sound as in *race*.

Underline and read aloud the word *upon*.

Once upon a time, a boy named Lance went out to pick up sticks. His mom gave him nice red mittens in case his hands got cold.

"Take the mittens and keep them safe," his mom said. But as Lance left, he ran fast and lost a mitten at the edge of the wide forest.

Shared Read

 Underline and read aloud the words *so* and *happy*.

Talk about why the mitten puffed up a bit.

Five mice saw the mitten. "This is a nice place to rest," they said. So the happy mice went in and rested.

Then, a rabbit raced by. "This is a nice place for hiding," she said. So the rabbit went in and hid. The mitten puffed up a bit.

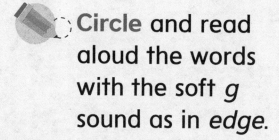

🔍 **Find Text Evidence**

✏️ **Circle** and read aloud the words with the soft *g* sound as in *edge*.

👥 **Talk** about what has happened to the mitten so far. Make a prediction about what will happen to it next.

Next, a hedgehog came sniffing by. "This is a nice place for taking a nap," he said. So the hedgehog went in and slept. The mitten puffed up a bit more.

Just then, a big bear came by. "This is a nice place to get warm," he said. So the big bear went in. The mitten puffed up from all the animals in it. It puffed up as much as a mitten can.

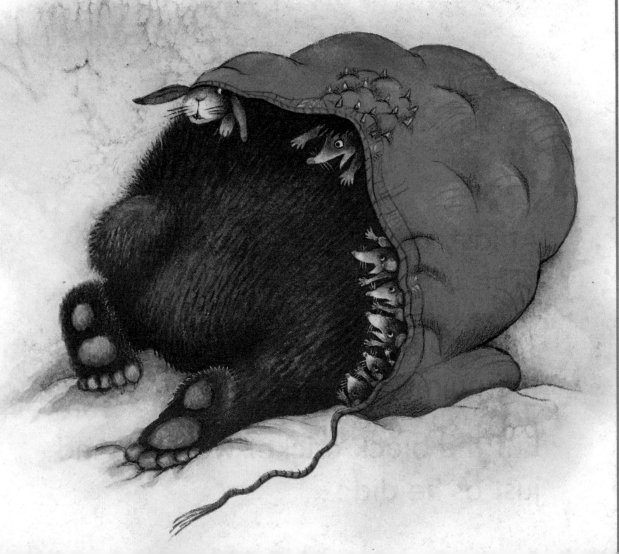

Find Text Evidence

 Talk about what happened to the mitten. Did you predict this?

 Retell the story using the pictures and words from the story.

At last, a black cricket came by. "This is a nice place," he said.

"We do not have any space," said the animals in the mitten.

But the black cricket went in. And just as he did . . .

Rip! Snap! POP!

When Lance came back, there was not a trace of red mitten left. So sad!

A **folktale** is a genre. A folktale is a story that has been told for many years. Folktales may have animal characters that act like people.

 Reread to find out what makes this story a folktale.

 Talk about the words "Once upon a time." What do they mean?

 Write two clues from the story that show it is a folktale.

Folktale Clues

The **plot** is the series of events that happen in a story. A **cause** makes a plot event happen. An **effect** is the event that happens.

 Reread "The Nice Mitten."

 Talk about causes and effects in the folktale.

 Write the causes and effects.

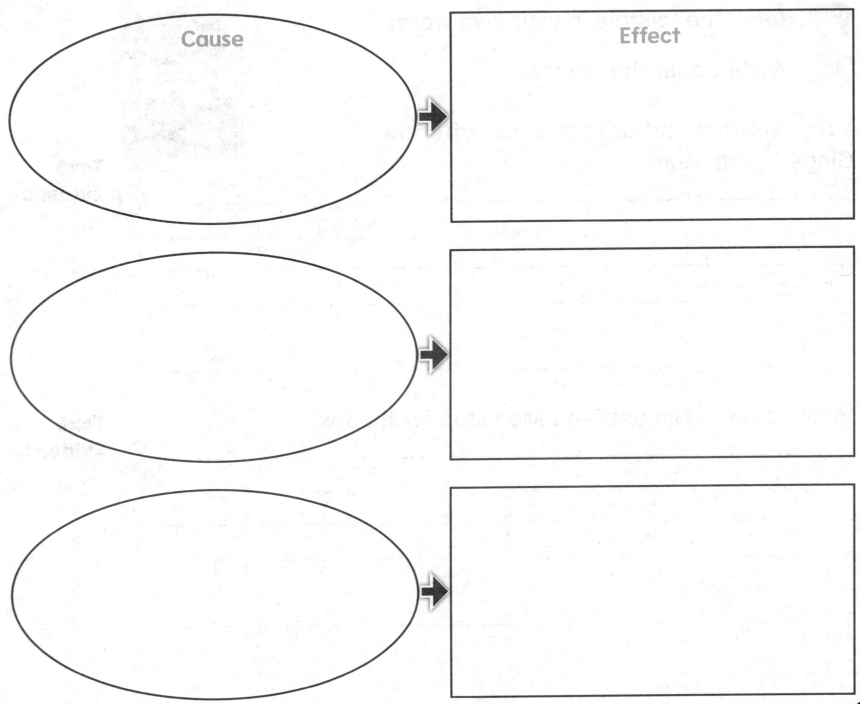

Cause

Effect

Read

Respond to the Anchor Text

Retell the folktale in your own words.

Write about the folktale.

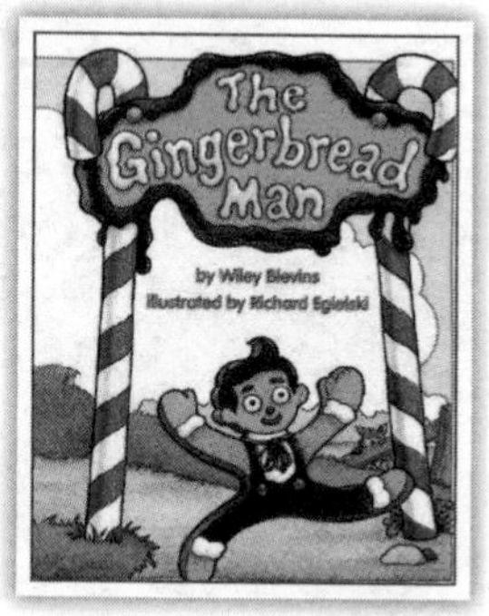

Why do Gram and Gramps chase after the Gingerbread Man?

Text Evidence

Page

Why does the Gingerbread Man stop for the fox?

Text Evidence

Page

Talk about how the folktales are the same and different. Speak in complete sentences.

Write about the folktales.

What happens to the mitten and the Gingerbread Man at the end of each story?

_____

_____

_____

_____

What other folktale characters does the fox remind you of?

_____

- -

_____

_____

- -

_____

Quick Tip

Think of words to describe the fox.

The fox is . . .

This reminds me of . . .

Talk about which words repeat on
pages 56 and 61.

 Write the sentence with repeating words.
Then read it aloud with your partner.

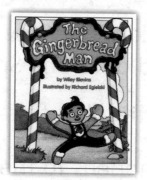

How do the repeating words affect the story?
Share your answer.

Talk about what happens when the Gingerbread Man meets the cow and the duck on pages 57–59.

 Write about each event.

Gingerbread Man Meets Cow	Gingerbread Man Meets Duck

What do you notice about the pattern in the story?

_____

- -

_____

- -

_____

Talk about what happens when the Gingerbread Man meets the fox on page 61.

Write about the event.

Gingerbread Man Meets the Fox

How does the pattern in the story change?

_____

_____

_____

_____

 Write About It

Imagine that the Gingerbread Man decided to run around the lake. Write a new ending to the story.

Mother Goose Rhymes

Higglety, Pigglety Pop

Higglety, pigglety, pop!
The dog has eaten the mop.
The pig's in a hurry.
The cat's in a flurry.
Higglety, pigglety, pop!

 Read to find out what Mother Goose rhymes are like.

 Underline three lines that end with words that rhyme.

 Read aloud the poem. Clap your hands to the beat. Talk about the rhythm you hear.

Hey! Diddle, Diddle

Hey! diddle, diddle,
The cat and the fiddle,
The cow jumped over the moon;

The little dog laughed
To see such sport,
And the dish ran away with
the spoon.

 Underline and read aloud the word that rhymes with *moon*.

 Talk about why the dog laughed.

Quick Tip

Reading the poem aloud can help you find the rhyming words.

Talk about how the poems make you feel.

Write and read aloud the rhyming words from each poem.

Higglety, Pigglety Pop	Hey! Diddle, Diddle

How do the rhyming words affect the poems?

_____

_____

_____

Talk About It

Think of more words that rhyme with *pop*. Then think of and talk about a rhyming line to add to "Higglety, Pigglety, Pop."

All About a Folktale

Step 1 **Find** a folktale you have never heard or read. Look online or in books.

Step 2 **Read** or listen to the folktale.

Step 3 **Write** the title of the folktale. Then write what it is about.

_____

- -

_____

- -

_____

_____

- -

_____

_____

- -

_____

Step 4 Write why you think people have been telling the folktale for years and years.

_____

- -

_____

- -

_____

- -

_____

- -

_____

Step 5 Choose how to present your work.

Talk about how the wolf might trick the girl in the picture.

 Compare the characters in the picture to the characters from *The Gingerbread Man*.

In *Little Red Riding Hood,* the wolf tries to trick the girl.

What I Know Now

Think about the folktales you heard and read this week. Write what you learned about folktales.

_____

- -

_____

_____

- -

_____

_____

- -

_____

 Think about what else you would like to learn about folktales. Talk about your ideas.

 Talk about your favorite folktale from this week. Tell why it's your favorite.

Talk About It

Essential Question How is life different than it was long ago?

Talk about what these children from long ago are playing with.

 Write how playing long ago was the same as playing today. How was it different?

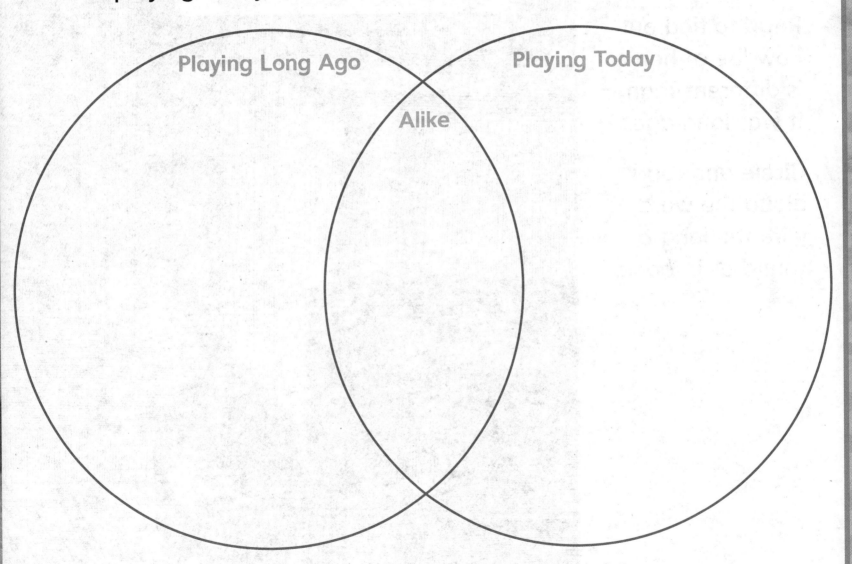

Playing Long Ago

Playing Today

Alike

Fox Photos/Stringer/Hulton Archive/Getty Images

Shared Read

Find Text Evidence

 Read to find out how life at home is different than it was long ago.

Circle and read aloud the word with the long *o* sound as in *bone*.

Essential Question

? How is life different than it was long ago?

©North Wind/North Wind Picture Archives

Life at Home

Shared Read

Find Text Evidence

 Underline and read aloud the word *people*.

 Think about what you just read. Do you understand it? Reread to be sure.

Has home life changed a lot since long ago?

Yes, it has!

Long ago, many families cooked, worked, and slept in one room.

Today, families can live in large homes that have lots of space.

A long time ago, homes had just one room. People ate and slept in that same room.

Today, homes can have many rooms.

Panorama Productions/Alamy

Shared Read

 Circle the words with long *u* as in *cute*.

 Talk about how people used to cook. Reread and use the picture if you are not sure.

How did people cook and bake long ago?

A home had a brick fireplace with a pole. A huge pot hung on this pole. People cooked in this big pot.

Long ago, there was an oven at the side of the fireplace. Bread was baked there.

Today, stoves can use gas or electricity.

Now, we use a stove
to cook and bake things.
We still use pots.
But these pots are not
as big as that old pot!

(t) William King/The Image Bank/Getty Images; (b) Stockbyte/Getty Images

Shared Read

✏️ **Underline** and read aloud the words *boy* and *girl*.

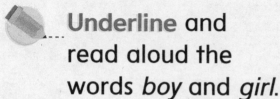 **Talk** about helping out at home long ago and today. Which was easier?

Back then, kids helped out a lot. A boy helped his dad plant crops. A girl helped her mom inside the home. She made socks and caps. It takes a long time to make those things.

A spinning wheel was used to spin wool into yarn.

Today, people buy most of the things they need and want.

Now, we shop for things such as socks and caps. We shop for things to eat, as well.

But kids still help out at home.

Find Text Evidence

 Talk about why washing dishes is easier today. Reread and use the pictures if you are not sure.

Retell the text using pictures, photos, and words from the text.

Back then, people got water from a well. Then they filled up a big tub and washed things.

In the past, people washed dishes in a tub made of wood.

Now, people can wash things in a sink. We can wash dishes in a dishwasher, too.

Life is not as hard today as it was long ago!

Today, it's easy to wash dishes in a sink or dishwasher.

Hero Images/DigitalVision/Getty Images

A **nonfiction** text gives information and facts about real people and real things.

 Reread to find out about the real things this nonfiction text tells about.

 Talk about what this text tells about.

 Write about two real things in the text. Then write what you learn about them.

Real Things	What I Learn

When you compare, you think about how things are the same. When you contrast, you think about how things are different.

 Reread "Life at Home."

 Talk about how homes long ago and today are alike and different.

 Write about homes long ago and now.

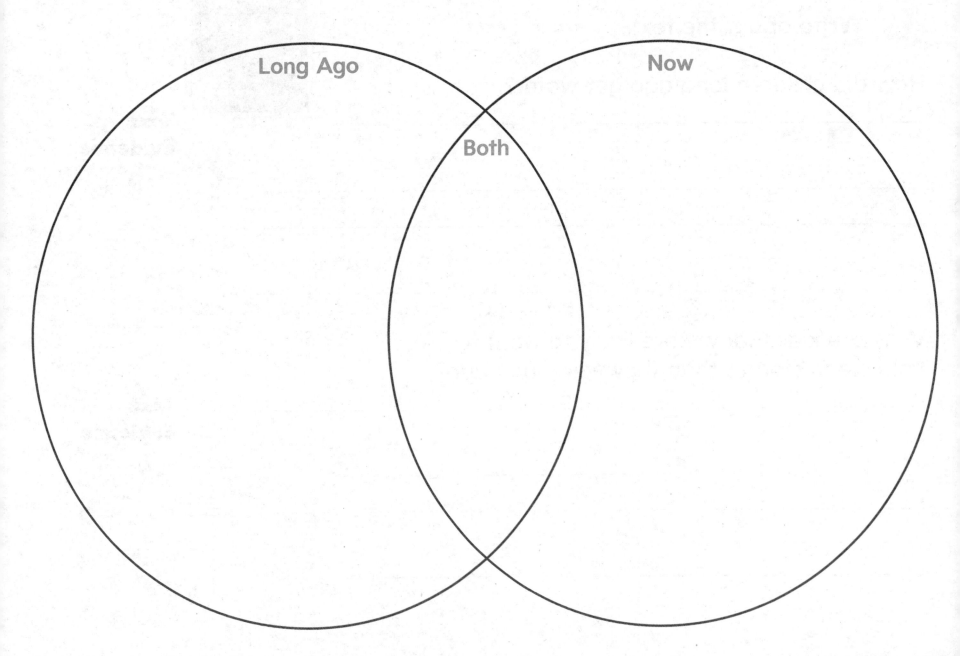

Long Ago

Now

Both

Retell the text in your own words.

Write about the text.

How did children long ago get water?

_____

- -

_____

- -

_____

Text Evidence

Page

Why are kids today more likely to want to help clean clothes than they were long ago?

_____

- -

_____

_____

- -

_____

Text Evidence

Page

Talk about how the texts are the same and different.

 Write about the texts.

What do these texts compare?

_____

- -

_____

- -

_____

What do kids still do today that they did long ago?

_____

- -

_____

- -

Combine Information

As you read each text, think about how your ideas change.

First I thought kids today and long ago . . .

Then I thought . . .

Talk about what you learn from the text on pages 76–77.

 Write about the images on pages 76–77.

Page 76	Page 77

How does the author organize the information?

_____

_____

_____

Talk about what you see in the photos on pages 78–79.

 Write what the photos show.

Page 78	Page 79

How do the photos help you understand the information in the text?

_____

- -

_____

- -

_____

Talk about the details on page 80.
Then talk about the details on page 81.

Write details from the text and photos.

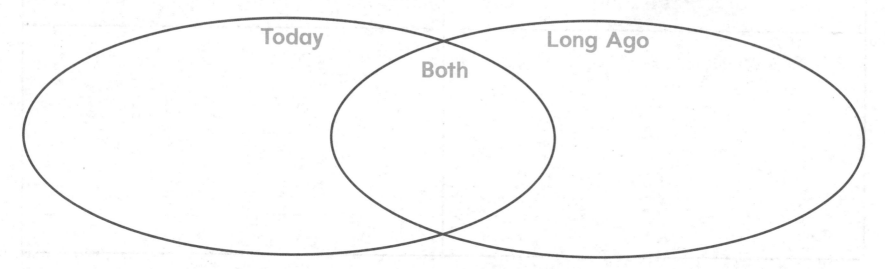

Today   Long Ago

Both

What do you understand because of the way the author organizes the information and details?

_____

- -

_____

_____

- -

_____

Write About It

Is being a kid better today, or was it better in the past? Use evidence from the text.

From Horse to Plane

People today can go places in cars, planes, and trains. Long ago there were not as many kinds of transportation. Before engines, people had to walk or use horses.

 Read to find out how transportation has changed.

 Circle the words that tell how we can go places today.

 Talk about what changed transportation.

Library of Congress Prints and Photographs Division (LC-D41-891)

Then the train was invented. Years later, cars were invented. Soon, the airplane was invented.

Airplanes can go over mountains and oceans. Today we can go across the world in a day. That could take years long ago!

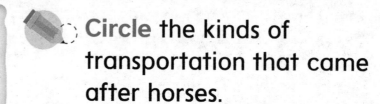 **Circle** the kinds of transportation that came after horses.

 Talk about how airplanes changed travel.

Quick Tip

Use these sentence starters:

Airplanes help people...

This is important because...

Bettmann/Getty Images

Talk about the information on each page.

 Compare how people went places long ago and now.

Long Ago	Now

Why is "From Horse to Plane" a good title for this text?

_____

- -

_____

- -

_____

Talk About It

What does the author want you to learn from reading this text?

Schools Long Ago

Step 1 Pick a teacher or an older person at school to ask about his or her school life as a child.

_____

- -

_____

Step 2 Write your questions about how school life used to be different from today.

_____

- -

_____

- -

_____

_____

- -

_____

Step 3 Ask your questions.

Step 4 Write what you learned about how school used to be different from today.

_____

- - - - - - - - - - - - - - - - - - -

_____

- - - - - - - - - - - - - - - - - - -

_____

_____

- - - - - - - - - - - - - - - - - - -

_____

- - - - - - - - - - - - - - - - - - -

_____

Step 5 Think about how to present your work. You may choose to create a recording of your interview or make a poster of a school from long ago.

Talk about what the children in this photo are doing.

 Compare the photo to the text *Long Ago and Now.*

Quick Tip

Compare the photo and text using these sentence starters:

In the photo...

In Long Ago and Now...

What I Know Now

Think about the texts you heard and read about now and long ago. Write what you learned.

_____

- -

_____

- -

_____

- -

_____

 Think of what else you would like to learn about life long ago. Talk about your ideas.

 Share one thing you learned this week about nonfiction texts.

Talk About It

Talk about what the man in the photo is doing.

 Write your ideas about what happens to tomatoes after they are grown.

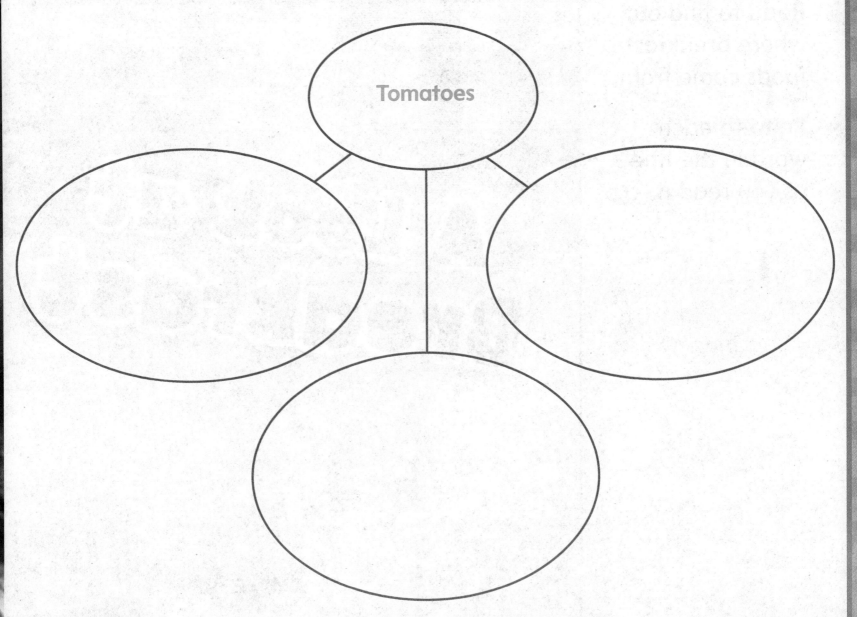

Tomatoes

Find Text Evidence

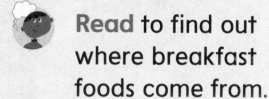

Read to find out where breakfast foods come from.

Point to each word in the title as you read it.

Essential Question

How do we get our food?

A Look at Breakfast

Find Text Evidence

 Circle the words with the same vowel sound as in *look*.

 Make sure you understand how flour is made. Reread page 126 if you need to.

Bread is good for breakfast. But this isn't bread yet. It is wheat. Flour will be made from the wheat.

The wheat is crushed to make flour.

Bloomberg via Getty Images

First, dough is made. Next, the dough is shaped and baked. Then, it is done. It is bread. Last, the bread is put in bags.

Shared Read

 Find Text Evidence

 Circle the words with the same vowel sound as in *look*.

Underline and read aloud the words *every* and *after*.

Grape jam is good on bread. But this isn't jam yet. It is a grape vine full of grapes.

Grapes grow on vines and then are picked when they are ripe.

Alberto Nardi/AGF RM/age footstock

Trucks take the grapes to a plant. Every grape is crushed to make mush. After that, the mush is cooked. Now, it is grape jam. Yum!

Shared Read

 Make sure you understand what happens at a plant. Look at the photo and reread page 131.

 Talk about the steps for making orange juice.

Orange juice is good for breakfast, too! Lots and lots of Sun makes oranges big and ripe. They will taste good. Soon, the big, ripe oranges will get pulled down.

White Star/Monica G/imageBROKER/age fotostock

Trucks take piles and piles of oranges to a plant. Then, they get washed. Next, they get crushed. Big sacks get filled with juice.

Shared Read

Find Text Evidence

Underline and read aloud the words *buy* and *work*.

Reread any parts you do not understand before you retell the text.

The food is shipped in trucks to shops. It is stacked up. Now, it is for sale. People will buy it and bring it home. It will make a good breakfast!

It takes work to make food for breakfast.

Food	Where It Comes From	How It Is Made
bread	wheat	Wheat is crushed into flour. Dough is made. Dough is baked into bread.
grape jam	grapes	Grapes are crushed to make mush. Mush is cooked into jam.
orange juice	oranges	Oranges are crushed into juice.

(bkgd) Artur Marciniec/Alamy Stock Photo; (t) D. Hurst/Alamy; (c) C. Squared Studios/Photodisc/Getty Images; (b) Stockbyte/Getty Images

Nonfiction gives facts about real things. It uses photos to give more information.

 Reread to find out what makes this a nonfiction text.

 Talk about what you see in the photos.

 Write two facts from the text. Then write what else you learn from the photos.

Facts from Text	Information from Photos

Authors often give information in sequence, or time order. Words such as *first, next, then,* and *last* help you understand sequence.

 Reread page 127 of "A Look at Breakfast."

 Talk about how bread is made.

 Write the steps the chef uses for making bread on page 127.

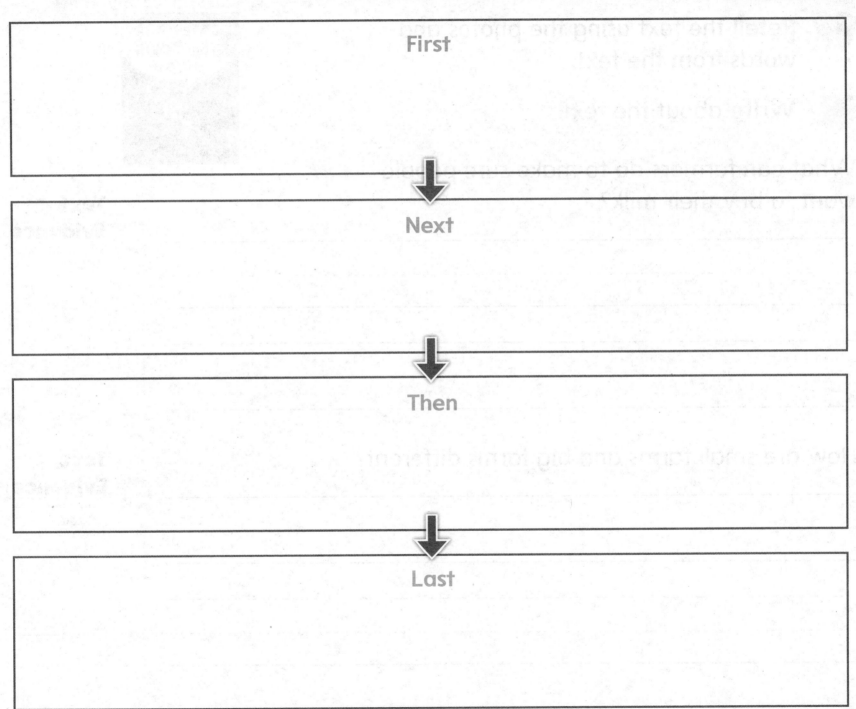

First

Next

Then

Last

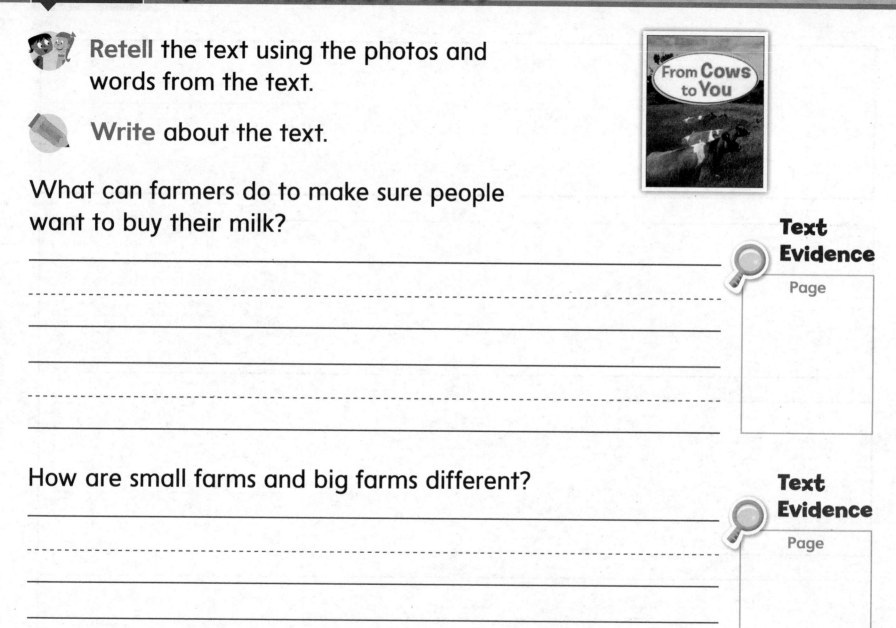

Retell the text using the photos and words from the text.

Write about the text.

What can farmers do to make sure people want to buy their milk?

Text Evidence

Page

How are small farms and big farms different?

Text Evidence

Page

 Talk about how the texts are organized. Speak in complete sentences.

Write about the texts.

How are these texts the same?

_____

- -

_____

- -

_____

Where does food come from? Use evidence from both texts.

_____

- -

_____

_____

- -

_____

Quick Tip

Compare the texts using these sentence starters:

"A Look at Breakfast" tells how . . .

From Cows to You *tells how . . .*

Both texts tell how . . .

Talk about what you see in the photos on page 96.

 Write what the text says about the photos.

I see . . .	I read that . . .

What do the photos help you understand?

_____

- -

_____

- -

Talk about the information on pages 96–99.

Write details from the text that answer the questions.

What is this text about?	How does the author organize the information?

What does the author want you to understand about milk?

_____

- -

_____

_____

- -

_____

Write About It

Which job in the milk process would you like to have? Why?

A Food Chart

Dairy is one food group. The other food groups are grains, fruits, vegetables, and protein. A healthy diet must have food from every group.

 Read to find out about the food groups.

 Circle the words that tell the five food groups.

 Underline the sentence that tells what a healthy diet has.

JGI/Jamie Grill/Blend Images/Getty Images

Do you eat food from every group? This chart can help you find out.

Five Food Groups

Dairy	Grains	Fruits	Vegetables	Protein
milk	bread	apples	lettuce	egg
cheese	rice	bananas	carrots	nuts
yogurt	pasta	oranges	broccoli	meat

 Circle your favorite food in the chart. Tell which food group it belongs to.

 Talk about what the chart teaches you that the text does not.

Talk About It

Why did the author include a food chart?

(tl) PhotoObjects.net/Getty Images; (tcl) IT Stock/PunchStock; (tc) I. Rozenbaum & F. Cirou/PhotoAlto; (tcr) I. Rozenbaum & F. Cirou/PhotoAlto; (tr) Isabelle Rozenbaum & Frederic Cirou/ PhotoAlto/ Getty Images; (c) Comstock/Jupiter Images; (clc) Ildi Papp/YAY Micro/age fotostock; (cc) Ingram Publishing/age fotostock; (crc) Comstock/Jupiter Images; (cr) I. Rozenbaum & F. Cirou/PhotoAlto; (bl) Ingram Publishing/SuperStock; (bcl) Stockbyte/SuperStock; (bc) Stockbyte/Getty Images; (bcr) McGraw-Hill Education/Mark Steinmetz, photographer; (br) ami mataraj/Shutterstock.com

Research a Food Item

Step 1 Choose a food to learn about.

_____

- -

_____

Step 2 Write questions about where your food comes from.

_____

- -

_____

- -

_____

- -

_____

Step 3 Use tables of contents to find the information you need. Read for answers to your questions.

Step 4 **Write** what you learned about your food.
Put the information in the correct sequence.

First

Next

Then

Last

Step 5 **Choose** how to present your work.

Talk about the painting. What does it tell you about where olives come from?

 Compare the olives in the painting to the grapes used in jam in "A Look at Breakfast."

Quick Tip

You can compare using these sentence starters:

Olives come from . . .

Jam is made from . . .

They both . . .

This painting shows workers picking olives.

Courtesy National Gallery of Art, Washington

What I Know Now

Think about the texts you heard and read this week about how food gets from the farm to your table. Write what you learned.

_____

- -

_____

_____

- -

_____

_____

- -

_____

 Talk about what else you would like to learn about how we get our foods.

 Share one thing you learned this week about nonfiction texts.

Writing and Grammar

Danica

I wrote a nonfiction text. It is about real things and events.

Nonfiction

My nonfiction text has facts and information.

Student Model

Wrist Watches

People did not always wear wrist watches.

How did people check the time long ago?

They had to dig watches out of their pockets.

Blend Images/Shutterstock

But soldiers needed to check the time quickly.
So they tied watches to their wrists. It's much
easier to check the time with a wrist watch!

 Talk about what
makes Danica's
text nonfiction.

 Ask any questions
you have.

 Circle a fact about
something real.

Plan

Talk about ideas for your nonfiction text.

Draw or **write** about the ideas.

Quick Tip

As you brainstorm ideas, think about topics you are interested in and know a lot about.

Choose a nonfiction topic to write about.
Choose something you know about.

_____

- -

_____

Write facts about your topic.

_____

- -

_____

- -

_____

- -

_____

Circle what makes your text nonfiction.

Writing and Grammar

Draft

Read Danica's draft of her nonfiction text.

Organization

I began with the topic. Then I wrote more about that idea.

Student Model

Wrist Watches

People did not always wear wrist watches.

They had to check the time a hard way.

They had to dig watches out of their pockets.

But soldiers needed to check the time.

So they tied watches to their wrists. It's much easier to check the time with a wrist watch!

Compare and Contrast

I compared how people checked the time before and after wrist watches.

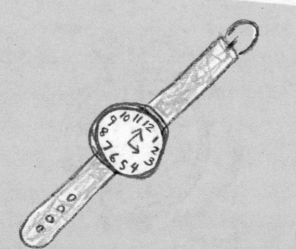

Your Turn

Begin to write your nonfiction text. Use your ideas from pages 150–151. Include details about your topic.

Writing and Grammar

Revise and Edit

Think about how Danica revised and edited her nonfiction text.

I revised by adding a question that my text answers.

Student Model

Wrist Watches

I spelled high frequency words correctly.

People did not always wear wrist watches.

How did people check the time long ago?

They had to dig watches out of their pockets.

I made sure to use past-tense verbs correctly.

I revised by adding a detail to give more information.

Grammar

- Verbs are action words.
- Verbs can be present-, past-, or future-tense.
- The verb *is* tells about one noun. The verb *are* tells about more than one noun.

But soldiers needed to check the time quickly. So they tied watches to their wrists. It's much easier to check the time with a wrist watch!

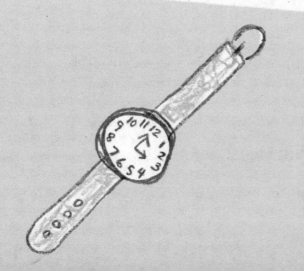

Your Turn

Revise and edit your writing in your writer's notebook. Be sure to use verbs correctly.

Share and Evaluate

Publish

 Finish editing your writing. Make sure it is neat and ready to publish.

 Practice presenting your work with a partner. Use this checklist.

 Present your work.

Review Your Work	Yes	No
Writing		
I wrote a nonfiction text.	☐	☐
I included details to tell about my topic.	☐	☐
Speaking and Listening		
I listened carefully.	☐	☐
I spoke when it was my turn.	☐	☐
I shared information about my topic.	☐	☐

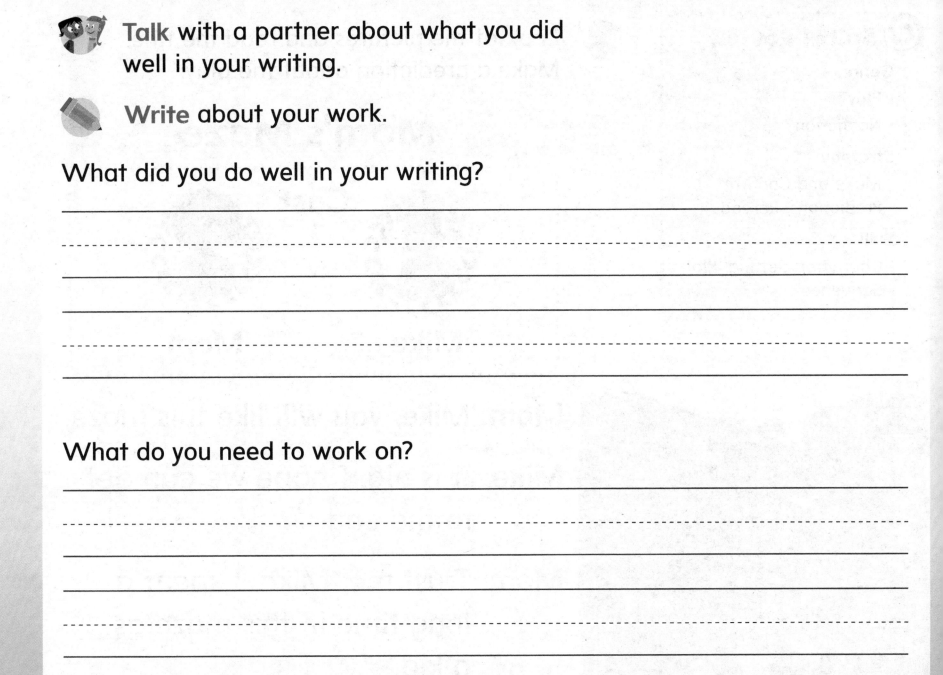

Talk with a partner about what you did well in your writing.

Write about your work.

What did you do well in your writing?

_____

- -

_____

- -

_____

What do you need to work on?

_____

- -

_____

- -

_____

Show What You Learned

⊙ Spiral Review

Genre:
- Play
- Nonfiction

Strategy:
- Make and Confirm Predictions, Reread

Skill:
- Character, Setting, Plot; Sequence

 Look at the pictures and read the title. Make a prediction about the play.

Mom's Maze

 Cast

Mike   **Mom**

Mom: Mike, you will like this maze.

Mike: It is big. I hope we can get to the end.

Mom: Trust me, Mike. I spent a long time in this maze as a kid.

Mike: But Mom, I think we passed this spot five times.

Mom: This maze is not like it used to be.

Mike: I will look past that big hedge.

Mom: That did it! Good job, Mike. We are at the end.

Mike: Now, I have spent a long time in this maze, too!

Show What You Learned

Circle the correct answer to each question.

1 How can you tell the story is a play?

   A It has characters who use dialogue.
   B It has animal characters who talk.
   C It has characters who could not be real.

2 Mike and Mom pass the same spot five times because —

   A the maze has no way out.
   B the maze is smaller than it looks.
   C the maze has changed.

3 Mom brings Mike to the maze mainly because she —

   A thinks Mike will like it.
   B needs help to get out of it.
   C wants to be outdoors.

Quick Tip

To understand Mom's actions, think about what she says at the beginning of the play.

Read "From Pup to Dog." Reread any parts you do not understand.

From Pup to Dog

Are pups just little dogs?
No. Pups can't do the
same things that dogs can.
Pups can't stand up.
Pups can't see well.
Pups can't smell much.
What can pups do, then?

Akkalak Aiempradit/Shutterstock.com

Pups nap, nap, nap. Pups drink milk, too. Napping and drinking help them grow.

After a while, pups can stand and see and smell.

Then pups can eat, and not just drink milk.

Soon, pups play. Pups nip and yap and jump around.

At last, cute pups grow up to be dogs.

Grigorita Ko/Shutterstock

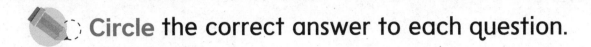 Circle the correct answer to each question.

1 How do you know this is a nonfiction text?

A It has dialogue.

B It is about a real animal.

C The events could not happen in real life.

2 When do pups eat food?

A Pups eat food as soon as they are born.

B Pups eat food before they can see well.

C Pups eat food after they can stand up.

> **Quick Tip**
>
> Look for words in the text that tell when pups can do things.

3 What do pups do when they are first born?

A They sleep a lot.

B They play a lot.

C They bark a lot.

Focus on Plays

A play is a genre. Plays are stories that are meant to be performed. Plays have dialogue, or words that characters speak, and a setting.

 Reread *The Big Yuca Plant.*

 Talk about what makes this story a play.

Write about the play.

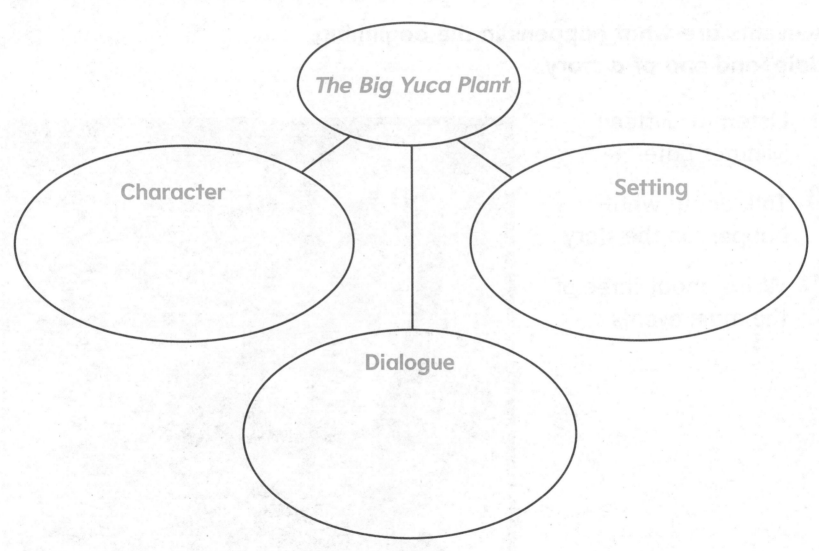

The Big Yuca Plant

Character

Setting

Dialogue

 Talk about how plays are different from other stories.

Extend Your Learning

Respond to the Read Aloud

The **events** are what happens in the beginning, middle, and end of a story.

 Listen to "Fifteen Minutes Late."

 Talk about what happens in the story.

 Write about three of the main events.

1. _____

2. _____

3. _____

Expand Vocabulary

Remember that verbs are action words, such as *wave, run, smile, see,* and *play.*

 Talk about when to use action words.

 Label the actions you see in this picture from *The Gingerbread Man.*

 Use each action word in a sentence.

Some other action words are *break, surprise,* and *hide.*

 Draw a picture that shows one of these action words. Then share your work.

Extend Your Learning

Make a Calendar

A calendar lets you see what is happening each day.

 Create your own calendar. Include pictures and words to show special days or events.

 Talk about the information you included in your calendar.

 Share your work with the class.

January _____

Reading Digitally TIME FOR KIDS

Online texts may have sidebar features that you can click on. Listen to "Seasons Bring Change" at my.mheducation.com. Click the sidebar features.

 Talk about the sidebar features.

 Write what you learned.

_____

- -

_____

_____

- -

_____

_____

- -

_____

_____

- -

_____

Write a Thank-You Note

A **thank-you note** is a short letter you write to say thanks.

 Look at and **listen** to this thank-you note.

The **greeting** tells who the note is for. →

Write what you are thankful for in the **body** of the note. →

The **closing** tells who the note is from. →

Dear Lucy,

Thanks for coming to my party.

I like the funny calendar you gave me.

Thank you!

From,

Ezra

Talk about someone you want to thank.
Then write a thank-you note. Write neatly.

Dear _____,

From,

Extend Your Learning

Choose Your Own Book

 Tell a partner about a book you want to read. Say why you want to read it.

Quick Tip

Try to read a little longer each time you read.

 Write the title.

_____

- -

_____

 Write about the book. What was it about? Did you like it? Why or why not?

Minutes I Read

_____

- -

_____

- -

_____

- -

_____

What Did You Learn?

Think about the skills you have learned.
How happy are you with what you can do?

I understand character, setting, and plot.	😊	😐	🙁
I understand sequence.	😊	😐	🙁
I understand how to compare and contrast.	😊	😐	🙁

What is something that you want to get better at?

_____

- -

_____

- -

_____

My Sound-Spellings

Aa a — apple

Bb b — bat

Cc c ck k — camel

Dd d _ed — dolphin

Ee e ea — egg

Ff f ph — fire

Gg g — guitar

Hh h_ — hippo

Ii i — insect

Jj j dge ge gi_ — jump

Kk c k ck — koala

Ll l _le — lemon

Mm m — map

Nn n kn_ gn — nest

Oo o — octopus

Pp p — piano

Qq qu_ — queen

Rr r wr_ — rose

Ss s ce ci_ — sun

Tt t _ed — turtle

Uu u — umbrella

Vv v — volcano

Ww w_ — window

Xx x — box

Yy y_ — yo-yo

Zz z _s — zipper

th	sh	ch tch	wh_	ng	a ai_ ay a_e ea ei	i y i_e igh ie
thumb	shell	cheese	whale	sing	train	five

o oa ow o_e _oe	u u_e _ew _ue	e_e ea ee e _y ie _ey	ar	er ir ur or	oar or ore	ow ou
boat	cube	tree	star	shirt	corn	cow

oi _oy	oo	oo u_e u _ew ue ou ui	a aw au augh al	air are ear ere
boy	book	spoon	straw	chair

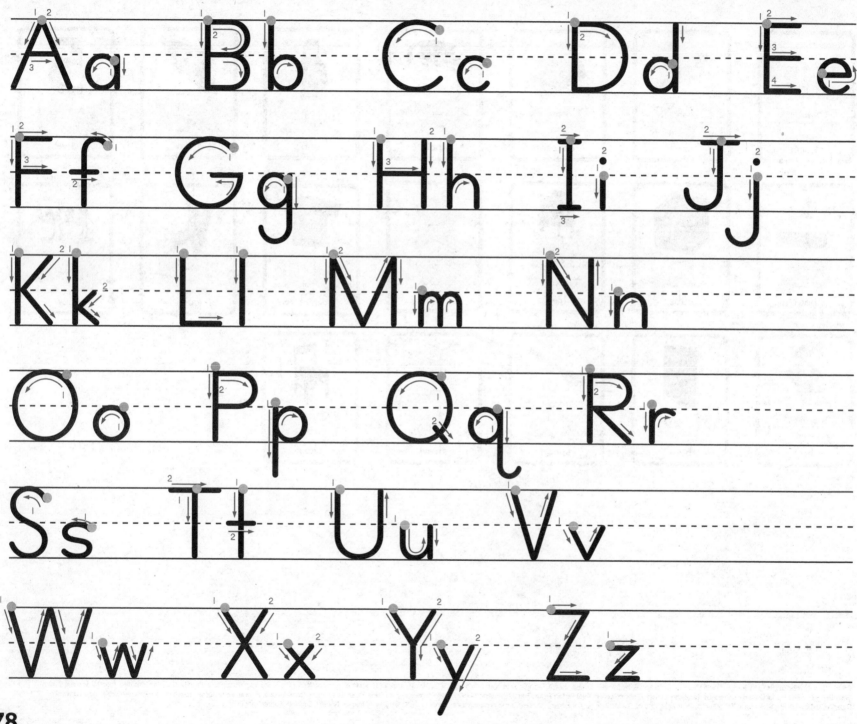